# THE HOUSE
# THAT *LOVE* BUILT

By

LORRAINE HALE

*Dedicated*

*to my mother,*

*"Mother Clara Hale,"*

*and the hundreds*

*of precious children*

*we have loved*

*at Hale House.*

# TABLE OF CONTENTS

Introduction

Epilogue

# INTRODUCTION

A while back, I sat at the dining table of Hale House watching the children gleefully fishing alphabet noodles out of their soup between bites of buttery grilled cheese sandwiches.

It's a scene I see so often—the children's happy laughter—Mother Hale fussing over them—a tipped over glass of milk—the clean plates and indifference to dessert.

But on this night, I saw it all much differently, like a stranger, looking at their beautiful faces for the first time.

I look at Jimmy with his big bright eyes and mischievous grin. His mother hadn't called here since the day she dropped him by all covered with cigarette burns and bugs, last January. One of our wonderful volunteers is taking him home weekends. His life is only 25 months old, but I could write a book on him alone.

Then the twins caught my attention, Sandy and Selena. Sandy is as perky as a kitten, Selena conversely slow and dazed. Their mother is out there somewhere pregnant again and still drugged out, refusing help. I wish I could help her, but for now, it's just these babies. Oh, these sweet little girls— but that's another book.

I continued looking around the room. And each child I saw reminded me of yet another story that needed to be told.

As I mentally began writing notes for this book,

I realized it would not be an easy book to read. All of the babies with whom I've met have had horrible beginnings.

Like you, I have compassion for the mothers, for in many ways they too are victims. For when we were not paying enough attention to the needs of the poor and dysfunctional, they were physically reproducing themselves. Their hundreds grew into thousands, these thousands into hundreds of thousands. Today millions who, relatively speaking, are poorer than ever before, more dysfunctional than ever before, and today too many are carrying the scourge of deadly diseases. The stories of the Hale House children could as well be those of their mothers and fathers. I believe it's called social reproduction.

Each of these little babies has stolen a part of my heart. Twenty-two years is a long time to care for babies, and I'll admit, some of the details are fuzzy. Names and faces have blended through time and as I look back, a few come quickly to mind, perhaps because of the unique way they arrived, or their pain, or their joy in living. It is those I wish to share with you in this small book.

I know that God has been very good to mother and I, because we have had the honor of caring for some of the most wonderful children on earth. You know, Mother Hale has a saying, "If you can't hold them in your arms, please hold them in your heart."

It is my prayer that through these pages you will grow to know and love these babies, as I do, and begin to "hold them in your heart."

God bless you for taking the time to read our little book.

# CHAPTER ONE

# A DIVINE APPOINTMENT

It had been a lovely day, weather-wise. Warm but pleasant. I just wished I felt the same about my career. My mind churned over the events of the day; another frustrating one working with the New York City School System.

I'd stopped by to see my mother, Clara Hale, before heading home. She gave me some lemonade and a listening ear. And in her usual manner, she gave me gentle but straightforward advice. Actually, it was the same advice I'd heard all my life. As I waited at the red light, I could hear her voice as clearly as though it was coming from my car radio.

"Lorraine, God put you on this earth for a reason. He's going to reveal that reason to you. Just wait. And keep your heart open so you'll see it when He puts it in front of you."

"I wish it could be soon," I said out loud, talking back to the voice in my head. "But I feel as if I'm not helping children."

"Look at me," I muttered to myself, "I went to college because I wanted to work with children. I care a great deal about children. I've spent years working days and going to college in the evenings to earn my undergraduate and graduate degrees in education and child development. And then all those hours researching and writing for a doctorate degree."

I shook my head in dismay and confusion. My monologue continued, "I want to make a difference in the lives of children, but how, how?"

About that time the light changed. As I was about to make a left turn, I noticed a woman sitting on a wooden crate just on the edge of the curb. It appeared she was nodding off with a bundle in her arms. I had seen this scene so often, I usually saw—but didn't see. Then I noticed the bundle jerk and I thought I saw a tiny arm.

The brown car behind me blew its horn, and startled me back to driving. My car inched ahead as I thought about the frightening possibility that the nodding woman was responsible for the care of a baby.

One block passed...then two...three...four. Abruptly, I made a sharp right turn, forgetting to signal. Back down the street I went...block one...two...three...four. Back to 146th Street, and the mother and baby came back into view.

Little did I know that in those few moments, I had done far more than redirect my car—I had redirected my life and the lives of my family. Not to mention hundreds of babies. But that is getting ahead of my story.

I parked the car and watched the woman holding the baby. She was in a deep nod. I feared the baby might slip out of her arms and onto the hard sidewalk.

"Excuse me, are you all right?" I asked the woman. I asked several times with no response.

Finally she looked up.

She struggled to focus on my face. I knew the look. She was on heroin and really out of it. It had been the drug of choice in Harlem for the past fourteen years according to authorities.

"You need some help with the baby," I said. "My mother will help you. She loves babies and it would give you a chance to get yourself together."

I pushed a paper with Mother's address on it into her frail hand.

"Here, go to this address. It's down the street and my mother will help you with the baby," I said, pressing the paper into her hand. "Her name is Mrs. Hale. The children call her 'Mommy Hale.' She is a short gray-headed lady that used to always have six or seven kids with her of all races. Just tell her her daughter sent you."

Having done my duty, I got back into my car and headed home.

Mother called me the next morning.

"Lorraine, there is a junkie at my door and she said you sent her," Mother said quickly, with sharp deliberation in her voice.

For a moment, the event of the day before escaped me. I took a deep breath. "Mother, I don't know any junkies...," I said without remembering.

"Then please explain to me where she got this note with my name and address written in *your* handwriting..."

"Oh, Mother," I said slowly, "I can explain. I'll

be right there."

Driving to her apartment, I was uncomfortable. Mother was terribly put out with me. I'd forgotten to tell her, darn it. Her reaction was unusual. It was second nature to both of us to minister to, rescue, and love babies.

By the time I arrived, the mother had left the baby...but she returned just a few hours later, demanding that Mother give her child back to her.

In no uncertain terms Mother told her, "Look here, I've raised my own children, I don't need yours to raise. Now you straighten yourself up and raise her yourself. You're this baby's mother!"

Without replying, the woman walked out the door, gripping the baby close to her.

The day passed, and although we both reflected on the ugly scene that morning, we had a good visit. Some hours later, we heard the doorbell ring. There the woman stood, visibly shaken and tearful, back with the baby.

Her words were slurred, but she was trying hard to sound straight.

"My baby. She's, she's..."

Toothless, her face grimaced. Tears filled her eyes.

It was a mixed cry for help, perhaps. But I could hear the deep anguished cry of a mother totally overwhelmed.

The baby's mother left quickly down the stairs—too uptight to take the elevator—before we could get anything from her.

Mother closed the door and walked into the kitchen, holding the baby in one arm. She started stirring oatmeal as if nothing had happened.

"She's gone," Mother stated softly.

"What's the baby's name?" I asked.

"I don't know," Mother replied.

"How old is she?" "I don't know," was the same reply. "How long are you keeping her?"

"I don't know," Mother said once again.

"Well, what do you know?" I asked, wondering if I'd have to "go fishing" all day to get some information out of her.

"I know you have to get a second job in order to help take care of this baby, Lorraine."

That beautiful little girl—we called her Amanda—became the first drug-addicted baby we ever cared for.

Overnight, Mother, then 65, abandoned any thought of "retirement plans" and became known as the "special lady" who would care for babies of drug addicts. Within three months her apartment was lined wall to wall with cribs for 22 infants. By then, I knew this would be my future as well.

Never could I have anticipated the impact of my impulse that warm spring day. It would forever change the lives of Mother, myself, and hundreds of babies. Babies born into this world with uncertain futures because of their mothers' drug abuse and addiction.

Thus began Hale House Center for the Promotion of Human Potential, Inc..

I often think of Mother's words: "Lorraine, God put you on this earth for a reason. He's going to reveal that reason to you. Just wait. Be still and listen with your heart so you'll know when He puts it before you."

God had revealed that reason to me. I understood that He had put Mother on this earth to care for these children, and I was here to help her help them.

Clearly, He has placed us here to help these precious innocent little ones know His kind of love.

Love that is more enduring than the long weeks of comforting them through the nightmare of drug withdrawal. Love that's bigger than the fear of HIV virus. Love that enables us to care for those infected with AIDS or syphilis.

Thank God, we were there for that heroin-addicted woman sitting on that milk crate on the street corner. To think if I'd missed that divine appointment, little Amanda might never have survived to be the lovely 22-year-old she is today. . . and there might never have been a Hale House.

And to think of all the smiles and sloppy kisses I would have missed on the faces of His children.

# CHAPTER TWO

## SHEER LOVE / TOUGH LOVE

We nicknamed him "Tiny Ty." His birth certificate listed him as "Baby Boy X."

Angels must have caught him the night his drug-addict mother pitched him in the dumpster. It was filled with broken wine bottles and splintered furniture. Yet he fell on the one soft thing in it; a piece of discarded carpet that smelled of wine. Fortunately, only a few mosquitoes and roaches had bothered him.

He was brought to us naked and with his umbilical cord still attached. It was truly a miracle that he had beaten the odds of dying from exposure those critical first hours of his young life.

And now he needed us to help him beat a more determined foe: heroin, his birth companion. The "monkey on his back."

I looked in his tiny face, and my heart broke. Though tiny for a newborn, everything about him was perfect. He grasped my finger with a strength that surprised me and his huge brown eyes seemed to boldly declare "Look out world, I'm here to stay!"

Ty was the eighteenth baby to come to Hale House that first year. Like the seventeen before him, we held him and loved him through the horrors of heroin withdrawal. Because he was so tiny and frail, we often feared we'd lose him.

But "Tiny Ty" beat the heroin.

And from that point on he kept us at a gallop. He didn't stay tiny. How could he—I've never seen a child eat more cereal than that one! Any kind, any brand, any time of day, just as long as we'd fill his bowl, he'd empty it and fret for more.

Oh, yes, he grew! He was crawling weeks before most babies his age, then he literally skipped walking and went straight to running. By the time he was returned, at fourteen months, to his grandparents, his new nickname was "Tyronne the Tank."

That was 1969. It was two years later that Hale House received its initial grant from the Office of Economic Opportunity. We continued to grow and in 1973, we incorporated to become Hale House Center for the Promotion of Human Potential, Inc., offering the first and only program in the United States for drug-addicted babies.

Mother and I established Hale House Center as a residential facility for children born addicted to heroin, alcohol, and various other drugs. We were definitely "a first." No one had gone before us to show how it was done.

I must admit, what we lacked in experiential know-how we made up for with the greatest of all gifts one human can give another: love. It was sheer love, administered to these tiny victims of drug abuse, that brought miraculous results.

I'm talking about the kind of love that outlasts weeks of torture a baby goes through while ridding its body of drugs received in the womb. I don't believe the world's best written explanation could fully relay to you what it's like for an infant going through withdrawal. It's heart-wrenching.

Fevers and tremors rack their tiny frames. They have constant diarrhea and vomiting. The endless hours of screaming day and night deny them any real sleep.

Patient love, persistent love, unconditional love. The kind of love the faithful have that never ends. It was all we had to offer them; it was everything we had to offer them.

As we saw these drug-addicted babies through their withdrawal, we found ourselves with drug-free babies who still needed a home that provided all the basic necessities. Many of the mothers were still abusing drugs and either unable or unwilling to take their children.

We had become licensed under the New York State Department of Social Services in 1973 and, simultaneously, a New York City voluntary child-care agency. It was a decision made for us. We went in reluctantly, screaming and kicking, because we knew there were no statistics or information available on how to care for these children. Yet, the bureaucrats would impose existing rules and regulations not appropriate to these babies and their parents' specific needs. All we knew to do was pour love and affection into their lives.

The longer we worked with the children, the more we realized we had to offer them an environment that included providing intervention in the early stages of development.

Along with this step we began a diagnostic and evaluation program for the assessment and care of these high-risk children. We enlisted the services of a psychologist, occupational therapist, and speech pathologist. We also taught the staff and volunteers how to interact with the children, how to teach them manners and social skills. Appropriate remedial programs were developed and we provided an on-going assessment of each child's progress.

While heaping unlimited amounts of love on the children we take in, tough love is what their parents encounter. Tough love in the form of rules. We don't pass judgment, but we enforce regulations. Any addicted mother whose child comes to Hale House has to agree to a drug-rehabilitation program before she can be reunited with her child.

Hale House's ultimate goal has always been to reunite families, but only when we know and can prove to the Child Welfare Administration in New York City that the child will be returning to a drug-free home.

We work with government agencies and professionals, as well as volunteers, in helping these mothers turn their lives around and get their families back together. Unfortunately, and for obvious reasons given the mothers' lifestyle, we rarely have the opportunity to interact with the fathers of these children. Therefore, our programs are primarily geared towards helping the mothers.

Our success rate has always been impressive.

Even when a mother has been unable to take back her child, there has often been a willing and capable grandmother. For a while cocaine/crack lessened our successes, but we are finally learning how to better handle these cases. However, when a parent refuses to plan to take the child and there are no known family members, we place the child with an adoptive family as soon as possible.

The greater portion of this book is dedicated to sharing case histories of children who have called Hale House "home." It was difficult choosing from the some 800 plus stories I have to pick from. I genuinely wish I could share them all because each is unique.

Every child that has come our way has left his or her indelible mark on our lives here at Hale House. Their tears, laughter, first steps and final good-byes have all made us the most blessed people for having been touched by their young and sometimes brief lives.

As you read this short book, take my mother's advice. Keep your heart open, so you'll see what it is God wants you to do.

We need you to help us continue the wonderful work of Hale House...

The work of loving children. The work of lifting lives out of garbage dumpsters...literally, like "Tiny Ty" and figuratively, by saving families being "trashed" by drug abuse.

Hale House has and will continue to make a difference as long as caring people don't throw away their conscience and ignore the needs of these children.

Come with me and meet some of our other "treasured friends."

*what have i done*
*so wrong*
*to deserve*
*so cruel*
*a welcome*
*from womb to world*

*where is this thing called bonding?*
*a mother's tender embrace*
*for me, her "pride and joy"*

*i only know her bondage*
*in its worst way*
*its "kiss"*
*that sears my body with*
*pain*

*Mommy, Mommy*
*have i been so bad*
*you had to*
*punish me*
*before you*
*ever*
*saw*
*me*

# CHAPTER THREE

## SHARRI

"Would you look at that face," I said to Frances, our veteran cook, "she's got the two deepest dimples I've ever seen." And her hair was a shock of silky ringlets.

For sure, babies didn't come more adorable than this brown-eyed beauty. But neither did they come as much in need. Sharri was a gorgeous child but she was also a victim of a maternal drug addict.

Her mother had injected heroin just hours before Sharri's delivery. A full twenty-four hours after her birth, this beautiful infant was twisting and thrashing wildly. Her struggle was harrowing.

Sleepless days and nights were filled with life threatening fevers, cold sweats and violent tremors. Her chronic diarrhea would constantly rob her body of what fluids we could get into her by bottle. That is, what she didn't manage to throw up.

At least we could rotate off and on caring for her, but she never got a moment's reprieve from the torture of coming off heroin, cold-turkey. Today, some hospitals give such babies methadone or paregoric to ease their suffering. But at Hale House we deal with the after-effects.

So it means hours, days, nights, and weeks of holding, rocking, soothing, bathing, loving and praying for these innocent victims of their mothers' thoughtless actions. Doing everything we can to help them live through the nightmare that grips them.

The only thing that seemed to calm Sharri was to hum the tune to "Hush, little baby, don't say a word, Momma's gonna buy you a mockingbird." When you hummed that tune, Sharri's little body would relax enough to allow her a few deep breaths before another wave of spasms hit.

Sharri's nightmare lasted five days and nights. It took two and a half months to stabilize her. We later realized the severity of her withdrawal was due to her mother's use of an extremely pure quality of heroin throughout her pregnancy. In those days, the term "monkey on my back" referred to your drug habit. Sharri's monkey was the size of King Kong.

But once through it, a precious little person emerged. Her ringlets reminded me of Shirley Temple. Animated, talkative, and loving, she captured hearts in a heartbeat.

My favorite story on Sharri is the time a cricket found its way into the children's sleeping quarters. How a cricket found its way to the inner city of New York City, I'll never know, but somehow one had arrived at Hale House. From day one, it would sing all night from a hiding place. During the day, it would show itself but always manage to avoid capture.

Seeing the adults in hot pursuit of the elusive cricket, Sharri would join the search with great intensity. Then at night when it would start its rhythmic chirping, Sharri just could not sleep.

She'd stand up in her crib and enthusiastically repeat "'icket... 'icket... 'icket."

The two of them would chirp back and forth for hours before she'd fall asleep. After a week of their nightly duets, the chirping stopped. It was a month later, dear "'icket" was found caught on the inside of the air duct.

Sharri was about fourteen months old at that time. Her mother only visited her once a month. Then the visits became more frequent—weekly. Later she told us that after several near overdoses, she realized she wanted to live for herself and her daughter. She entered a drug rehabilitation program and, against great odds, completed the program and became a "recovering addict."

When we were confident of her determination to "stay clean" and her ability to take care of Sharri, mother and daughter were reunited.

The morning they left together was a hallmark day for Sharri and her mother. And it was a very "soggy" one for all of us at Hale House...despite the shining sun outside.

Today, both are doing very well. Sharri's a fourteen-year-old high school student and wants to be a photographer. Her mother is married and serves as a drug counselor for young women.

Two lives changed. Two lives destined to make a difference in this world. Because Hale House was there to help them find their way.

## THE WHITE HOUSE
### WASHINGTON

March 14, 1984

Dear Mrs. Hale:

It gives me great pleasure to commend you for the wonderful work you are doing on behalf of children of addicted mothers.

Your willingness to open your heart and home to these babies and to offer an island of hope to their mothers, has moved me deeply. I have shared your story with Nancy and I know that you have given us a great deal to think about. What a wonderful person you are and what an inspiration you are to others!

God bless you for your concern. You are truly one of His angels here on earth.

With respect, admiration and best wishes.

Sincerely,

Ronald Reagan

# CHAPTER FOUR

## MIGUEL

That cold spring morning was to be a landmark day at Hale House. Little five-day-old Miguel would fill the last available crib. His was the twenty-second one we'd been able to squeeze into Mother's tiny five-room apartment.

We'd noticed his mother the day before pacing the sidewalk in front of the apartment carrying her tiny bundle. But upon calling out to ask her in, she ignored us and hurried down the street. Now she stood at the door shivering in a halter top and miniskirt, holding a wailing infant wrapped in a faded pink towel.

"I hear you take care of babies," she nervously said in broken English, trying to make herself heard over the baby's cry.

"Yes, we do and there's room for one more. Please, won't you come in?" I asked her.

Echoing my invitation from the kitchen, Mother asked her to join us for a sandwich and coffee. We'd found that offering a bite of food or drink afforded us our best chance of getting needed information without making mothers feel threatened by direct questioning. Too often, we'd simply been handed an infant over the threshold without the mother telling us anything about herself or her infant.

Fortunately, she accepted but insisted she was in

a hurry and couldn't stay long. It was obvious her trembling wasn't merely from the cold but could also have been a sign of the onset of withdrawal. My guess was heroin, judging by the needle marks on her thin arms.

Stepping inside, she headed in the direction of Mother's voice in the back of the apartment. I followed her, taking time only to throw a diaper and blanket over my shoulder.

"Here, let me hold her for you," I offered, assuming by the pink towel it must be a girl.

Thrusting the bundle in my arms, she replied, "No, it's a boy. If it was a girl, then maybe I could keep the baby. His name's Miguel."

I opened the blanket to behold a round little face, crimson from crying. He was a newborn but looked like he already needed a haircut. Unwrapping him further, in order to change his diaper, he bellowed out a scream the volume of Tarzan's. He was definitely withdrawing from something.

Warming her hands on the cup of hot coffee, the mother gave her name as Olga. Her voice was shaky and steeped with frustration.

"I can't get him to take my milk and he won't stop screaming," she said. "And he doesn't act right. I can't afford a doctor and besides I'm sick myself."

She went on to explain the father was a dark Hispanic and her relatives hated him. They refused to accept a Black/Hispanic male as part of the family.

Even as she spoke, I thought, "How could anybody hate a baby? He didn't choose who his parents would be, what race, what color. He's just an innocent baby!"

Because my mother was a licensed foster parent, I'd grown up with forty foster brothers and sisters of all colors and backgrounds. And every one of them, just like you and me, had started life as an infant with the basic need to be loved and nurtured. Just like the precious child I held in my arms and just like the other twenty-one innocent babies living in that apartment.

Her earnest words brought me back to the conversation. "They won't let me bring him home. Please take him," she pleaded. "I'll let his father know he's here and he might be able to take him."

Abruptly she stood up, saying, "I gotta go," and began to move towards the doorway.

Still holding the screaming baby, I knew I had to ask the question before she left, "Are you on anything, any drugs?"

She turned, casting an expression of confusion and resentment. I quickly added, "It's okay to tell me. It's just so we know how to help the baby if he has any of it in his system."

Pondering the question for a few tense moments, she must have sensed my genuine concern. Hesitantly, she admitted to mainlining heroin. She also volunteered the information that the baby's father was into drugs, but not the heavy stuff.

Mother and I accompanied her to the door where

her parting words were, "I've heard good things about this place. And I believe if anybody can, you can find him a home where he's wanted, no matter what color his momma and daddy are."

Her eyes glistened with tears as she turned and ran down the stairs, not waiting for the elevator. We never saw Olga again.

I was so glad we didn't have to say no to her. Thank God we had one more crib left for Miguel. It was hard to believe it had only been two months since the first baby and now we had twenty-two.

With what information his mother had given us, we had a basic idea of what withdrawal symptoms Miguel would experience. Granted, we didn't have any medicine to ease his discomfort, but by being aware of his exposure to drugs in the womb, we knew he would need massive doses of love and patience from us.

He was an extremely handsome baby. Finally, drug free after three weeks, he developed a ravenous appetite. Feedings every four hours weren't enough for him. We had to supplement his diet with interval bottles.

I remember having to fight to hold onto his bottle as he drank from it. The force of his suction was so strong it appeared he could actually pull it right out of your hand. And he was the most cuddling baby. He always wanted to be in your arms.

And it wasn't a "hold me/spoil me" kind of demand to be held, but more of an intense hunger for love and human contact. It was as though we just couldn't fill up Miguel's love tank.

But that was okay. Between Mother and I, and the wonderful friends and neighbors who had begun volunteering to help us, we took turns holding him—and holding him—and holding him. And every minute was pure joy because he was such a loving child.

While we never saw or heard from Olga again, she was faithful to tell Miguel's father he was at Hale House.

Curious to see his son, he came to visit when Miguel was sixteen months old. He brought his aunt with him. A very short, stout woman, she was his father's sister. She was Puerto Rican and knew very little English. But the minute she saw Miguel she began to cry and repeat something over and over again in Spanish.

I asked Miguel's father what she was saying, and with a tinge of tearfulness in his voice he replied, "She says he looks just like my father when he was a little boy."

Regaining her composure, the aunt began a staccato discussion with her nephew. Finally, turning to me, he said what was music to my ears.

"My aunt is returning to Puerto Rico and knows my family will want Miguel. Can I have him so we can send him or can you help us get him home?"

Home—home! A family and relatives for handsome loving Miguel. Like his mother had said, "a home where he's wanted." I had to turn away to hide my own tears.

It took a few months to go through all the legal and logistic channels. The aunt visited often and Miguel bonded beautifully with her. Thankfully, everything fell into place for him to go with her to Puerto Rico.

I can still see Miguel dressed in his little blue shorts wearing a matching vest, white shirt and bow tie. He looked like a miniature banker, his vest doing its best to hold in his rotund tummy.

I watched as his aunt walked away to board the plane with him bear-hugging her neck as tight as he could. His brown eyes beamed as he waved "bye-bye" over her shoulder.

"Finally," I thought, "Miguel's love tank is full." And from the laughter I heard rolling back at me down that airport terminal, it was full to over-flowing.

# CHAPTER FIVE

## DELCIA

Delcia came to Hale House in the late '70s. The story of her arrival at Hale House rivals all others.

It was spaghetti night for the children and all hands were "on deck" to help feed our hungry crew. Spaghetti night is always a fun night with spaghetti and sauce slipping and sliding across plates and faces. The children love it. And well armed with washcloths and napkins, we adults enjoy their enjoyment.

But in our preoccupation we never heard the front door open or close. In a moment of partial silence as the children ate, we heard a faint cry that didn't come from within the dining room. It sounded like the muffled whimper of a puppy.

Ms. Jackie Edmond, a Hale House social worker since 1973, went to investigate.

"My word!" we heard her exclaim from the hallway. "Mother Hale, Dr. Hale, you won't believe what I'm looking at."

Mother and I cast reciprocal glances of "Who goes first?" knowing we couldn't both run out and leave the children unattended. As I was closest to the hallway, Mother motioned me on.

Rounding the dining room archway, I looked in disbelief. A baby was hanging on the inside of our front door. Looking like a parachutist caught in a tree, this sleepy infant, about 10 months of age, was suspended mid-air, the back of her shirt hung on the coat hook.

The poor thing was so tiny and weak, it couldn't even cry out in protest. So stunned at the sight, I forgot about Mother's turn to see. Though it couldn't have been but a few seconds, our stone silence drew her to the hallway.

"For heaven sakes! Get that baby down!" Mother's voice broke through our shock.

I supported her body weight as Ms. Edmond released the shirt, taking care not to scrape her back on the hook. The child felt like a hollow baby doll, she was so light.

A piece of paper was stuffed inside her clothes with the name "Delcia Staton" and her date of birth scrawled in pencil. Holding her in my arms, I was smitten by the delicacy of this beautiful piece of God's handiwork.

In no way making light of this blatant act of abandonment, yet so taken by the "little human gift" we had found "hanging" on our door, I quipped, "Well, Delcia thank you for dropping in. You're just in time for spaghetti night!"

Living in the inner city, we are very careful about keeping doors locked. As best we could understand it, the door's latch didn't catch as one of our volunteers left that afternoon. Though harm could have resulted from such an oversight I believe it was God's providence that prevailed, because Delcia proved to be nothing less than a blessing.

It was almost a year before we heard from

Delcia's mother and father. In that time she grew into a lovely little girl. Her dark lustrous hair framed a delicate face with almond-shaped dark chocolate eyes and a rosebud mouth. The only thing missing that would make her beautiful was a smile. Delcia wouldn't smile.

At first we thought she had a hearing problem or brain disorder, she was so unresponsive. Tests for both revealed no abnormalities.

A psychological evaluation suggested that she had been severely emotionally deprived as an infant. The chronic and intense deprivation of love and nurturing she experienced caused her to retreat into a world of silence and indifference. In essence, her emotions had shut down.

With the help of the child psychologist and speech therapist who work with Hale House, the staff was instructed on how to deal with Delcia's emotional needs. Her case was severe, but not hopeless.

Daily doses of gentle hugs and endearing kisses were her "emotional vitamins." And before or after I kissed her, I would try to get her to make eye contact. Or maybe I'd say something affirmative like, "Delcia, I love you," or "You are so special to me!"

All the children receive daily "emotional vitamins," and for most it is enough to be affirmed verbally or physically. But with Delcia it took the verbal and physical expressions together to try and reach her in her private world.

We saw her first smile when she was thirteen

months. Most children smile by their fourth month. Someone had brought a basket of puppies for the children to see and touch. Although the children had seen grown dogs in the park, they had never seen the likes of these furry butterballs.

To avoid any tugs-of-war we allowed only as many children in the room as there were puppies. When Delcia's group came in, we had them sit in a circle and, as usual, Delcia dropped her head, folded her hands and stared into her lap. One by one we gave each child a puppy.

I placed hers in her lap. She didn't move, but kept her hands tucked tightly against her tummy. While all the other puppies were squirming and scamping about, this little fella seemed tired and was content to just nuzzle in her lap.

Then something magical happened. Slowly, Delcia unfolded her hands and began to pat the puppy. It was like watching something in slow motion, seeing her tiny hand lift and fall ever so gently across his fur.

Then the miraculous happened. It must have been the wetness of his nose or sandpaper tickle of his tongue, but as he began to lick her hand, she smiled. Delcia smiled. And with each lick and nuzzle, her smile got bigger and bigger.

Now, I'm not one to give certain children privileges over others. But, I have to confess, I arranged for Delcia to have extra helpings of "puppy love" that day.

From that point on, she began to bloom. It was

as though that puppy had chewed through the ropes of rejection and despair that had bound her. Her emotional and social development began to make steady progress and eventually she caught up with her peers. (Incidently, we kept that puppy, a German Shepherd named "Cricket.")

Several months later, a visitor to Hale House noticed Delcia and fell in love with her. The woman was single and a school teacher who had already adopted one girl. She just had to have Delcia.

As customary, we desire to place children in adoptive homes, versus foster ones. This woman's intentions to adopt were clear and her qualifications were unquestionable. We arranged visitation privileges that expanded to outings together and eventually overnight visits. The prospects looked perfect that Delcia would soon have a mother and a home.

But three months into their relationship, Delcia's parents reappeared.

The mother had been in jail for illicit drug sales and the father was released from a psychiatric ward. One of their relatives had brought Delcia to Hale House and hung her on the back of the door.

The parents wanted her back, and in spite of their previous absence, we could not legally deny them their child. So we began to work with the mother to get her into a drug treatment program. Meanwhile, the father visited Delcia at Hale House.

(Licensed as a congregate child care center, we have our own Board of Directors, rules and regulations. But we still answer to New York City's child welfare system. There are no laws restricting parents from seeing their child once they've been released from mental institutional.)

In Delcia's case, the father posed no threat to her. The only noticeable peculiarity about him was he always wore bright green. Green pants. Green shirt. Green shoes. Everything green. Though his parenting skills were limited, he was very caring and loving towards her. However, other circumstances kept him from removing her from Hale House.

Sadly, it wasn't long before the mother was back in jail and the father recommited. There was hope again for Delcia's adoption. No sooner would we think it was okay to proceed, when one or other parent would appear wanting her back.

Thank God, the school teacher's determination never wavered. I must say, in all my dealings with parents, I have never known one as dedicated and self-sacrificing as this woman. Gratefully, the courts agreed and she was allowed temporary custody of Delcia.

Constantly in and out of their respective institutions, the parents contested the court ruling. But because of their inability to stay out of trouble long enough to establish a home for Delcia, the school teacher was finally allowed to adopt her.

From the day Delcia had won the heart of that school teacher to the day she was legally adopted, six long years had passed.

It thrills me to see children restored to their

parents, knowing there's a chance they'll make it as a family. But in Delcia's case, I was thrilled to see a new family created.

A family created out of the commitment and love of a woman for a little girl left hanging by her shirt on a door hook. Love that endured six years of fear, faith, and patient waiting to call that little girl "my daughter."

# CHAPTER SIX

## LET'S MAKE A DEAL

Think of a game show and picture this with me:

See a handsome game host standing beside an enthusiastic female contestant. The drum roll begins as the host's words vibrate from his microphone. Here come the famous lines..."And which one will it be? Door Number One? (fanfare)...Door Number Two? (more fanfare)... or...Door Number Three? (even more fanfare).

The audience is going wild. The contestant is in a state. She's wringing her hands, pulling her hair, biting her lower lip. Her face grimaces with uncertainty and confusion. All around her, voices hail the door of their choice.

Now, turn the page of your imagination and see with me:

A well-dressed (perhaps "decked out" would be more descriptive) man is standing on the street in the inner city project nearest you.

Beside him is his female contestant (rather, client). She lives on that street. Why, she was born on it, raised on it, and in all likelihood, will die on it.

Talking very low, (no mikes here) he makes his voice as titillating as the game show host.

"What'll be, hon?"

He's not asking her which door. She knows what's behind the doors of those that live in poverty.

Behind Door Number One, she knows there is a rat and roach-infested apartment . . . (in)complete with no father, just a single struggling mother trying to work at a job that can't cover the cost of day care, much less food and utilities.

So she locks the children in to go work all day. She leaves a four-year-old "in charge" of a two-and-a-half-year-old and an infant.

And then she knows that behind Door Number Two is a prostitute accommodating a customer. He is into the worst type of gratification, thereby forcing upon her the worst kind of degradation.

But, it's the only way she can make that kind of money, considering she didn't graduate from junior high school.

Finally, behind Door Number Three . . . now this has got to be where the prize is.

You're right!

Drugs! All kinds. It's a regular candy store. And each guarantees the great escape from all she knows around her; the feelings of being ugly and worthless compared to society's definition of beauty and success . . . and the feelings of abandonment and fear she knew as a child behind Door Number One.

Drugs provide her an escape from her conscience that replays violent and vile acts committed against her. They are an escape to a place where she is beautiful, dignified and . . . a perfect 10.

This game called life doesn't offer anything better than drugs to this un-parented, love-starved, uneducated and self-effacing girl/woman.

So she settles for Door Number 3.

And like the game show contestant, we see her wringing her hands (in desperation for another hit or fix). She pulls at her hair as waves of paranoia hit her. (She can't bite her lower lip, though, because it's too swollen from being hit in the mouth by her lover the night before.)

Her face grimaces ugly with pain as she pushes and pushes—

...out Poverty's next contestant.

And his name is...(no fanfare)...

Innocent Child Victim

alias...Baby Addict.

# CHAPTER SEVEN

## TIFFANY

I would prefer to tell only happy stories. But reality demands sharing the whole truth about what we see and experience here at Hale House.

Child abuse in the womb caused by a mother's drug use is what we see most often. And emotional abuse as shared in the story of Delcia is also common. There's no doubt all child abuse is horrible.

But seeing firsthand the results of deliberate physical abuse inflicted by a parent is something you can never prepare for. Even in the less severe cases, feelings of disbelief and nausea engulf you. The desire to rescue, protect, and love the child makes me feel like a mother bear defending her cub. And for the sake of emphasis, make that a large mother bear.

It is important, though, that while I admit having those feelings, I have learned that to love the child and hold animosity toward the parent is hypocritical. That's why we always tried so hard to get parents into drug treatment programs—and why we opened our own in late 1990.

It's also why we established Homeward Bound, a program for mothers who are completing their drug treatment and want to create a new life for themselves and their children. It provides affordable housing, and networking on parenting, and HIV support programs among other assistance to enable mothers and their children to stay together.

Hale House has its success stories, but we also have our very sad stories where justice doesn't prevail and children lose. They may lose the innocence of their childhood, a chance for a happy future, or even their lives.

In the case of a toddler named Tiffany and her infant brother, Thomas, we see both the success and failure of our efforts and those of government programs designed to help our nation's children.

Born to alcoholic parents, Tiffany and Thomas were frequently left alone for lengthy periods in a filthy apartment. When the parents were home, it was a place of considerable disorganization, confusion and violence. In addition to being neglected, they were not fed or clothed adequately.

Neighbors frequently heard their pitiful cries and finally, someone called the police. Upon arriving, they had to enter the apartment by force, finding three-month-old Thomas in a filthy crib, lying in his own excrement and completely covered by insects. Before they could change his diaper, they had to take him outside to shake off the roaches.

Tiffany, the two-year-old toddler, was dirty and had cigarette burns covering 30 percent of her body. Where there wasn't a burned sore, she had an insect bite.

This poor child had somehow survived by eating anything she could find on the floor, including roaches and cigarette butts.

Because Hale House was just around the block

from the apartment, the police brought the children directly to us. There is no word to describe their condition. Our first course of action was to bathe them. It still makes me shiver to remember.

They were filthy from weeks (if not months) of not being bathed. So when we got them in the tub, kicking and screaming, they were so afraid. Live roaches came out in the water as we washed their hair. It was so badly matted we couldn't see their scalp to know the roaches were there.

Having obviously suffered the greater abuse, Tiffany didn't know what it was to be lovingly touched. She cringed with fear even as we tried to put medicine on her burns and bites. Her eyes were those of a cornered animal, frightened to death, but prepared to strike.

Both children of an alcoholic mother, neither had the facial characteristics typical of Alçoholic Syndrome (i.e. taut eyelids, very flat bridge of the nose, low ears, and a very thin top lip).

Tiffany was very petite and somewhat pretty with a heart-shaped face and big eyes. However, she was a very difficult, withdrawn child, excessively willful, fearful and distrusting. She also showed marked developmental delays and was not the loving or lovable child the staff had come to expect. Her transition into Hale House was exceedingly difficult for her as well as the staff.

Little Thomas had more resiliency. Very much the cuddler and social initiator, he interacted beautifully with other children as well as adults. He was a handsome baby and, by all outward appearances, a happy well-adjusted child.

A major difficulty we had with both occurred every mealtime. In spite of his long and lean physical build, Thomas was a bottomless pit. You couldn't fill him up and he protested loudly when he was lifted out of his highchair.

And even at the age of two, Tiffany had never been taught how to use a spoon or how to sit at a table.

When her food was placed before her, she would grab it by handfuls and plop to the floor to eat it. After months of working with her, she stayed seated at the table but continued to use her hands as eating utensils; she then began to steal food off the other children's plates.

Perhaps saddest of all, she, like most children who have suffered from starvation, would hide food in her clothing to carry it to hiding places in the house. Until we caught on, there were many discoveries of "moldy" biscuits and cookies in the strangest places. The after-mealtime game with Tiffany was to check her pockets. Once she became used to the fact that there would be another meal, she loved our finds, laughing heartily as she gave us her treasures.

Four months after their arrival, Tiffany had begun to make progress adjusting to and accepting her new environment. It wasn't outstanding progress, but progress nonetheless.

Then we received a call from a case worker with

the Special Services for Children (SSC). He said he had located the children's maternal aunt, who after a little persuasion, agreed to visit the children. He thought he could eventually encourage her to take them.

The Hale House social worker, Ms. Edmond, was informed of the developments and agreed to help work out the details.

The maternal aunt called Hale House requesting visitation privileges. Our social worker eagerly granted her request and a visitation date was set.

On the day of the scheduled visit, Tiffany, beautifully dressed, waited impassively for the reunion. Finally, it came. The aunt and a friend, neither of whom Tiffany recognized, arrived...half an hour late.

We concluded that they were drunk because of their difficulty navigating through the halls and maneuvering themselves into chairs. Their slurred speech and the overwhelming, rancid odor of stale alcohol led us to suspect this was no isolated drinking celebration, but a common condition for both.

Still, as long as there was no obvious threat to the child, or drinking on the premises, we could not deny them their visitation rights. (This was the case at the time regarding drug users, but today, due to the violent nature of persons taking drugs like crack and cocaine, we have tighter visitation restrictions.)

The reunion was uneventfully eventful. Tiffany didn't talk, the aunt couldn't talk, and the friend wouldn't talk. After endless silence, the social worker suggested she bring Thomas down for his visit. That was rejected with a resounding "No! I'm only interested in her."

Immediately after they left, our social worker called SSC to discuss the aunt's visit. She was verbally reprimanded for alleging the aunt had been drinking.

Two visits ensured the level of contact remained the same without improvement or change. The SSC field worker was pleased with the aunt's consistency, and called to say she would take Tiffany permanently on the next visit. Concerned, our social worker asked about home conditions. She was told they had been found adequate.

The aunt came one Friday, the day of Tiffany's scheduled departure. As usual, she arrived very late and very drunk. She asked for a letter to welfare in order to put Tiffany in her budget. Unaware of any such arrangement, Hale House's social worker declined the request.

Instantly enraged, the aunt, becoming loud and vulgar, threatened not to take Tiffany unless these conditions were met. A call to SSC cleared up the misunderstanding, and the aunt left, taking a quiet, unsmiling, unresponsive two-year-old with her.

Two days later, Monday morning, the case worker from SSC called to ask if we could take Tiffany back. It seemed that during "Auntie's" weekend celebration of Tiffany's return to the care and loving concern of relatives, the apartment was set on fire and completed burned out.

We were told that Tiffany was emotionally distressed by the experience but physically unharmed. Several guests received minor burns. Immobilized by her "condition" at the onset of the fire, the aunt had to be removed from the burning apartment by the firefighters. She suffered second-degree burns and smoke inhalation.

As heartbreaking as it was, we were unable to take Tiffany back because the vacancy had been filled the day she left. As it was, we were already over our limit. Our license could be revoked if we housed more children than our ordinance permitted. We simply had no more room.

Tiffany was placed in a foster home that proved not to be the best environment for a child who had already experienced so much pain.

If only we could have said "Yes, there's still room for Tiffany at Hale House." If only there were enough places like Hale House for all the Tiffanys of the world. If only. . .

(Borrowing Paul Harvey's famous teaser, "And now, the rest of the story," read on to learn what happened to Thomas—the little boy who wondered if he'd ever find a mother to call his own.)

# CHAPTER EIGHT
## THOMAS

Hale House was the only home Thomas had ever known. Having been an infant at the time of his abandonment, he had no recall of the filthy apartment called "home" and people called "Mommy" and "Daddy" that Tiffany could remember.

From the start, Thomas attached to Mother Hale and she to him in a very special way. He loved to sit on her lap and be rocked, or trot along after her wherever she went. It never bothered her. Her supernatural reserve of patience, love and attentiveness for all the children never seemed to run out. And Thomas especially benefited from that endless supply of love Mother Hale had to offer.

We take great effort in meeting a child's emotional and physical needs during their time at Hale House. However, we consider it imperative not to interfere with the child's natural affinity for his or her parents. As caring people offer their time and energy as volunteers, each child is matched up with someone the child likes and who is willing to take the child on outings and weekend visits.

Our volunteers, as well as our staff, are cautioned not to allow a child to call them "Mommy" or "Daddy." (Note that Mother Hale is never called simply "Mother" but always "Mother Hale.")

Another reason for our caution is to keep the mothers from feeling threatened or displaced by the child's preference for someone else. This is crucial in building the mother's confidence in herself as the child's mother and also assures her our intentions at Hale House are to help her and her baby become a family again.

Of course you can't control a child's heart, and there are times they do prefer someone at Hale House. But our staff and volunteers try very hard to insure the greatest chance of success that mother and child will bond.

I would be remiss not to admit that this can be emotionally difficult for our staff and volunteers who have an enormous amount of love to give these children. And when his or her mother shows no interest in them, they can't help but get even more emotionally involved. It's only human.

Such was the case with Thomas. Initially, his mother made no contact whatsoever with Hale House. Except for putting out an all-points bulletin on her, we exhausted every avenue trying to find her. She had never been located and the Special Services for Children workers didn't press charges of abandonment and neglect after Tiffany and Thomas were found in the roach-infested apartment because she was never located. (Though through the "ghetto grapevine" we learned that she subsequently gave birth to three more children.)

Records revealed that Thomas and Tiffany's mother was the third generation of alcohol abusers, with concomitant emotional breakdowns, unemployment, poverty and violence. It was our guess she was among New York's growing army of nomads, living in one temporary shelter after another—anonymous, a permanent squatter, usually drunk.

Tiffany had been taken by the aunt only four months after arriving at Hale House. Though that effort to reunite her with a relative did not work out, she was subsequently adopted into a foster home. We hoped, for Thomas' own sense of self worth, he would be adopted with Tiffany or by another family as soon as possible. But he wasn't.

Instead, the months turned into years, and before we knew it, Thomas was almost four. He was a noticeably handsome little fella, 100% boy with just enough precociousness to keep you on your toes. But he had two strikes against his being adopted. He was a boy and also had very dark skin. For some reason, girls and lighter-skinned children are more readily adopted. It's a sad truth and terribly unjust.

But thankfully, there are many "color-blind" volunteers who love children just for who they are. Right after Thomas' second birthday, a wonderful man came to Hale House and offered to be a volunteer. Personality-wise, he and Thomas were a perfect match. Interestingly, the volunteer was white. Seen together, they created quite a visual contrast. But their obvious love and adoration of one another dispelled any contrast of heart.

Thomas had three best friends—Tony, Barbara, and Nellie. For the first three years of their lives they had been inseparable. They ate together, played together, comforted each other, rarely hitting, but always kissing.

As we hoped for their sakes, one by one Tony, Barbara, and Nellie left Hale House. But, oh, we were so sad for Thomas.

Tony was the first to leave. His grandparents decided they wanted him to live with them permanently. Thomas became melancholy. Typically a hardy eater, he lost his appetite and became willful.

A month later, Barbara left with an aunt who had finally gained custody. Thomas asked when he was going. We assured him it would be soon.

Ms. Edmond made another diligent effort to find someone related to Thomas, without success. We learned that his mother had given birth to another baby who was also in foster care. Once again she had disappeared without keeping in contact with any agencies.

During that time, Thomas' volunteer and Mother Hale did their best to lighten the heaviness of his young heart. But it was so much for a little boy to understand.

Granted, he still had Nellie, but her departure was imminent. With the absence of Tony and Barbara, Thomas' behavioral changes were apparent. He was often depressed, acted out, and was negative about most things.

In hopes of helping him through the loss of yet another member of the only family he'd ever known, Ms. Edmond took him for lunch to tell him that Nellie was away for the weekend. I was told he didn't say much.

Later, when alone with Mother Hale, he began to cry.

"What's the matter, Thomas?" Mother asked.

"I don't know," he muttered.

"It's alright to cry when you're sad," she reassured him.

"I know, I'm sad. Is Nellie coming back?"

"Yes! But she'll leave again soon. We're going to find a home for you, too, Thomas."

"I don't want to go. I want to stay here with Nellie and Tony and Barbara."

"They're gone, Thomas," Mother said.

"Then I'll cry. I'm sad."

Sensing his great pain, Mother replied, "Well, perhaps I'll cry also, Thomas."

The three other children were also experiencing separation anxiety. Tony had became withdrawn and constantly asked for his friend, Thomas. Barbara wanted to visit her friends and Nellie often reminded her new family she had to call Thomas.

With time, Thomas' anxiety did not lessen. A prevailing sadness seemed to snuff out his formerly bright disposition. His sadness was our sadness. The psychologist met with him twice a week.

A year passed with no prospects of adoption. Then, amazingly, his mother reappeared. This time the welfare agency was able to convince her to get her life together and get her children back. With Tiffany adopted, that meant Thomas and his two younger infant brothers, who were also in foster care, and the new baby in the mother's care.

Only a few months into her rehabilitation, she was granted weekend visitation with Thomas through the efforts of our social worker. Mother and I were uncomfortable about it, but Thomas went on his first weekend. Ms. Edmond called every four hours. On Sunday morning, after repeatedly calling and not getting any response, she went to the home.

As it turned out, the mother had been arrested on Saturday night. Both children were placed by the police in the custody of Special Services for Children (SSC). Ms. Edmond immediately tried to find Thomas, wanting him returned to the familiar and secure environment of Hale House. But, because of the red tape, it was three days before Ms. Edmond discovered his whereabouts.

Yes, we brought Thomas back, but the trauma he'd been through had already taken its toll. He was a different child. Once in a while, we saw a glimpse of the old happy, confident Thomas, but the Thomas that returned after just a few days absence, was confused, moody and willful. The loss of innocence.

His mother was released from prison and made a sincere second attempt to straighten out her life. Unfortunately, she failed again. Overwhelmed by the obstacles she faced, she convinced herself she couldn't succeed as a mother. So she gave the children up for adoption. She has had another child since that time.

Shortly after her decision, I spoke at a fund raiser for Hale House. In my speech, I interjected a humorous story about Thomas and his friend Tony.

The two had been allowed in the kitchen to watch Frances, our cook, prepare egg salad for a future meal. While her back was turned, one of them had managed to take an unshelled hard-boiled egg from the table.

Their "stolen treasure" undetected when they left the kitchen, the two devised a wonderful plan. They would take turns sitting on the egg until it hatched into a Golden Goose, like the one that laid golden eggs for the giant in "Jack and the Beanstalk." Once the goose was hatched and started laying eggs, they would share them only with their best friends and each buy a puppy of his own.

The discovery of the egg occurred weeks later "downwind" of the closet Tony and Thomas shared. Confronted by the aromatic evidence of their deed, Thomas turned to Tony and said, "I told you not to sit on it so long when it was your turn."

Following my talk, a couple came forward to thank me for my speech. They especially enjoyed Tony and Thomas' story and inquired about their situations. I explained the events of Tony going to live with his grandparents and the ordeals Thomas had experienced with the loss of his other friends and unsuccessful reunion with his mother. I added that he was still at Hale House.

As it turned out, that couple met Thomas and

wanted to care for him. They are all trying to adjust, but it has been very difficult and the future is uncertain. One of the saddest aspects of this story is that in all likelihood, Thomas, Tiffany, and their baby brother will never be reunited.

Pray for Thomas and Tiffany, and their three little brothers. . .that somehow, their tomorrows will be brighter and better than their yesterdays. And remember, too, their mother and their foster or adoptive parents. They all need our prayers.

Jamaica, New York
July 30, 1975

Mrs. Clara Hale
154 W. 122nd Street
New York, New York 10027

Dear Mother Hale:

It was March, 1972. There I was on 146th Street, with my son in my arms. Here, I was to leave my son with a person I knew very little about. But, I knew that I was like a blind person that needed a seeing-eye dog for guidance. As soon as I walked through the door there you were. You could hardly wait to get Adam in your arms. You were so warm and affectionate. You told me he would be alright, and not to worry. I felt so much better knowing Adam would be loved.

As months went by I came to see Adam. But, not as much as I should have. I was still in the process of getting myself together. Every time I saw Adam he was very happy, and I knew he loved everyone and was getting all the love and attention that a child needed.

I started picking him up on the weekends. I also started to understand my responsibilities as a mother to him. Lorraine gave me very good advice every

time I came to pick up Adam. I would leave feeling
stronger and knowing that I would have my son with
me very soon.

Then the day came when I should bring my son
home for good. I was so excited. When I walked into
the Hale House I became very sad. I realized I
would miss coming on Fridays to pick up Adam.
Not seeing Lorraine or you. Not being there to sit
and see the children running around laughing and
playing. I wanted to cry.

I can keep writing and never stop. Trying to express my feelings to you, Lorraine and your staff for
what you have done for my son and myself is very
hard to put in writing. I can say thank you a million
times but, I would never feel that I would be thank-
ing you enough.
Every Christmas you will receive a little something
from me always remembering you.

There were times when the "light at the end of the
corridor" was so dim, that success appeared impossible. But, as the saying goes "we shall overcome" and "we have," with your love and guidance.
Thanks, Thanks, Thanks........

Love always,
L.J.

# CHAPTER NINE
## CHLOE

It was August of '83 and as hot and humid as New York City can get. It's a known fact that crime goes up significantly during the hot weather months. Never had I seen so many women seeking refuge for their children and themselves from abusive husbands and boyfriends.

For every ten mothers that showed up on the steps of Hale House seeking refuge for their child we could only help one or two. We were always full.

I hated having to say, "I'm sorry, we just haven't any room." Turning away a woman, whether she's straight, drunk, or on drugs, but who is visibly bruised, bleeding, and pleading for safety for her baby, hurts us so much. Those we can't help are referred to various government agencies and shelters for battered women.

It was a sweltering late afternoon when we waved the final goodbye to nine-month-old Albert and his mother. Just as I had stepped into the welcomed coolness of my office, the doorbell began to ring furiously. Upon opening the door, a woman stumbled into the foyer. She was holding a baby splattered with blood.

Reading the startled look on my face, she quickly stated, "She's okay. I'm the one bleeding." Her voice was relatively calm considering her appearance. Her hair disheveled, clothes torn, and shoeless, she'd obviously fled for her life. The blood was coming from a cut over her eyebrow and a split lip that was swelling rapidly. The lip made her speech difficult to understand.

"My old man's messing with something bad. He got crazy on me again, third time this week. You gotta take my Chloe. Just for the weekend, that's all I'm asking," she pleaded.

She explained she had just left an older child with a relative but couldn't find anyone to take the baby. She needed to return to her apartment to get her things once she was sure her husband was gone. This beating had convinced her it was time to leave him.

We'd had to turn away four babies in the past three days. Now that Albert's crib was available it felt wonderful being able to say, "Yes, we can take her."

I invited her in and gave her an ice pack for her face while Birdie, a long-time Hale House childcare worker, took five-month-old Chloe for a much needed bath. A mature, wonderfully caring person, Birdie had Chloe cooing within seconds.

The mother's name was Reba King. (It's important to note that many of the women we deal with have very poor self-esteem. Abused by husbands or lovers, they usually receive little respect from anyone else, including personnel in emergency rooms and the various government programs they depend on. So as a means of fostering self-esteem in these women, instead of calling them by their

first name, we address them as Mrs. or Ms.) Ms.
Edmond took the necessary information from Mrs.
King, who promised to call us Monday as to when
she would pick up Chloe.

Other than getting herself mixed up with a bad
man, she appeared to be lucid and honest during
our conversation. But when we finally heard from
her the next Thursday (instead of Monday), there
was good reason to suspect she was "messing with
something bad" herself.

Sure enough, she not only went back home to her
abusive husband, but got high with him that very
evening. A phone call to Social Services, which she
had informed me was giving them financial aid,
verified her history of drug abuse.

It is not unusual for mothers to give us false information, but we know Hale House is really here
for the children. We do help the mothers, (though
they have a hard time accepting it) despite their initial fears. Given their lifestyle, many of them have
come to expect to be duped by lies and
manipulations.

But there were no regrets about getting involved
with little Chloe and her mother. It was obvious she
had some developmental delays, likely attributed
to exposure to drugs in the womb, but they weren't
extreme. Our occupational therapist was optimistic
she would catch up to her appropriate age level
within the year.

Comparatively chunky as babies go, Chloe was
really in pretty good shape physically. She wasn't

underweight or sickly like most of the children when they arrive at Hale House. Perhaps I hadn't been totally wrong in perceiving the mother as somewhat responsible.

Obviously, Chloe had been fed the right kind of food versus Coca-Cola in a baby bottle supplemented by potato chips, often the common fare for many of the children we see. Medical records provided by Social Services indicated Mrs. King had kept up with shots and check-ups for both children.

In spite of her developmental deficits, Chloe was a charmer. A bit of a manipulator, she could turn on the tears and turn up the volume of vocal protests at nap and bed time as quickly as she could coo and cuddle. When she laughed or smiled she had the irresistible charisma of an earthbound cherub.

Chloe was also our clown-in-residence. In typical baby fashion she would plant her head on the floor and walk her bottom up in the air becoming a human triangle of sorts. In that position her diaper made her top-heavy and she would flip flop over into an involuntary somersault. Of course, it made us laugh and clap at her antics, but even though she was so young, she did seem to connect our applause with her action.

Then when she began to walk we rewarded her efforts with glee and applause as you do with all babies. She somehow put two and two together and took to waddling a few steps, bending over, planting her head on the floor and doing one of her somersaults. The cleverness of her antics brought her so much applause it was as though she fell in love with the sound of it. So for the first three months Chloe could walk, to go from point one to point two had a certain rhythm. Four waddles, head on the floor, flip flop, four waddles, head on the floor, flip flop. From then on as soon as she'd wear out one applause-getter, she'd always come up with another one. Chloe was wonderful!

Her mother, Mrs. King, made sporadic contact with us, occasionally showing up for scheduled visits with Chloe. She wasn't an especially attractive woman but there was something very likeable about her.

She was aware of the ambivalent nature of her marriage. She loved the guy, but hated how he had allowed drugs to change him so much. In the beginning the two used them as a form of recreation. Her attitude towards drugs was to use them. Now she was seeing drugs using him. Their drug habit had begun as "user friendly" and turned "vicious controller."

Her husband hadn't been the violent type until he'd gotten heavily into crack. The more she saw him bound by his habit, the more she wanted to be free of her own. This type of reasoning for a drug addict is all too rare. She also dearly loved her children and wanted them back. The two incentives were enough to get her into a drug treatment program and she made excellent progress. The reuniting of Mrs. King and Chloe looked very promising.

Eighteen months after entering the drug treatment program, faithfully visiting Chloe and attending parenting-skills classes, Mrs. King was a different woman. No longer hindered by a poor self-image that kept her from believing she could change her life, she emerged into a confident determined individual. She'd even gotten financial aid to attend college and eventually receive a degree. She established herself in an apartment of her own and was pursuing a career (of all things) as a parole officer.

A month shy of her second birthday, Chloe left Hale House to live with her mother and five-year-old sister, Renee. It was a day of triumph for a woman whose maternal instincts, fortunately, had not been obliterated by drugs. Her victory was hard won and an admirable example of what determination and love can do in turning a life around.

I wish that was the end of the story. . . a happy ever after ending. And it almost was. Mrs. King did become a parole officer and, by report, a good one. But in a moment of weakness, she allowed her husband, now drug-free by his account, back into her life. She did not do drugs with him again. She was hoping she could influence him to stay clean.

Instead, their brief reunion as husband and wife resulted in her contracting HIV from him. He was unaware himself of having the disease at the time, and since HIV and AIDS were still relatively new to both the medical profession and public, neither of them knew the early warning signs of the disease.

By the time it was determined she had AIDS, she had been mis-diagnosed with "female trouble." When she returned to Hale House asking us to help her get Chloe adopted into a good home, she was the shadow of the woman I had known. She'd overcome so much, now to be beaten by a disease that defied a cure.

We did find a good family to adopt both Chloe and Renee. Their mother signed the release papers on her deathbed. She was thrilled they had been kept together. Shortly thereafter she died. The adoptive parents brought the girls to their mother's funeral.

More petite and reserved of the two, six-year-old Renee held tightly to the hand of her three-and-a-half-year-old sister. Chloe seemed unscathed by the solemnness that sliced through the silent gathering.

A small chapel, it was packed with people whose lives Mrs. King had touched as an empathetic and compassionate parole officer. She had been able to relate to others tempted or trapped by the tyranny of drug addiction. But she was also able to testify that there was a way to break free of that tyranny and find a new life.

I've often thought of her honest comment during a visit with Chloe. She was about halfway through her drug treatment program and we were sitting watching Chloe go to town on her favorite rocking horse.

In a philosophical moment she said, "You know, Dr. Hale, it sure is easier to go to hell than it is to get out of it.''

"Yes, I suppose it is," I mused with her. "From what I see of drugs, they're the Fast Express down."

"Yeah," she said with a faint laugh. "And coming out is the Slow Mo train up." Getting up to help Chloe dismount from her wooden thoroughbred, she looked straight at me and said, "But you know what? I'm going to make it, Doc. Slow Mo or not. I'm gonna make it, and so are my kids!"

Perhaps I've spent more time telling you a story about Chloe's mother than I have Chloe. But Mrs. King's victory was Chloe's victory. That mother left a legacy of what perseverance can do. Her story also exposes the deception that you cannot treat drugs as "recreational." Illegal drug use is addictive and destructive by its very nature.

I'll never forget Mrs. King and the gift she gave her children and me by being an overcomer, a winner, a woman who defied the odds and said, "I'm gonna make it, and so are my kids."

I'm indebted to her for showing me the strength that lies in the human spirit. Her example gave me hope to believe that potential strength lies in every drug addicted mother. When I want to give up on one of the women we try to help at Hale House through Homeward Bound, our counseling services and drug treatment programs, I think of Mrs. King.

Indeed, I consider myself privileged and proud to have known her.

## MOTHER HALE'S PRAYER

(for a baby with AIDS)


Dear Father in Heaven,
This baby will not live long
on this earth, but he will live
forever with you. Grant this
prayer that his remaining days
will be full of the happiness and
joy every infant deserves. Ease his
pain. Calm his fears. Chase away
his loneliness. Let him feel your
eternal love through me. Amen.

# CHAPTER TEN

## DANNY

In the seventies and early eighties we saw the majority of children brought to Hale House either return to their drug-free mother, or a caring relative, usually grandparents. But something began to happen to more and more children as we entered into the mid-eighties. It was baffling. It was heinous. It was crack/cocaine. It was AIDS.

The AIDS infiltration into the drug community actually began back in the late seventies. At least that would explain the deaths of many women we helped during that time. They would become sick, have their illness repeatedly mis-diagnosed (usually "female trouble," like Mrs. King in the previous chapter), fail rapidly in spite of medical intervention, and later suffer a tortuous wasting death typical of what we now know as AIDS.

Before AIDS generated the public awareness, as it has today, Hale House was seeing this insidious disease stalk and steal the lives of children and their mothers. Before AIDS we had hope for a certain amount of recovery for a child exposed to drugs in the womb. But since AIDS is not a drug, but a blood disorder, there is no "withdrawal" from it.

What is so sinister about AIDS, with regards to unborn children, is how it is transmitted. With the common practice of prostitution as a means of supporting a drug habit, women are especially vulnerable to exposure to AIDS through contact with multiple sexual partners who are infected. The added practice of drug addicts sharing dirty needles creates a second common way for women to contract AIDS. It's as though the unborn child of a drug addict doesn't have a chance against exposure to AIDS. It's almost certain to be exposed to it, one way or the other.

In addition to the devastating impact of AIDS, another wave of destruction swept the drug culture—the increasing use of crack/cocaine. Relatively cheap and easily available, it rapidly became the drug of choice.

A dark day had dawned on Hale House. A day that clouded our understanding of how to care for babies exposed in the womb to either crack or the AIDS virus. So little was known about both. Fear of the unknown (transference of AIDS) plagued our staff, as dedicated and caring as they were. It was the beginning of more sad endings to our stories.

The story of Danny is short because his life was so short. Though I knew Danny, the bulk of this chapter is his story as written by Tresmaine Rubain-Grimes, a graduate studies student who helped Hale House document the short and long term effects of drugs on children exposed to them in-utero (in the womb).

Deeply touched by Danny's brief life and a frequent contributor to Hale House's monthly newsletter, the "Mainliner," Tresmaine wrote the following story: "Fighting a Losing Battle: Danny's Story."

The last segment of the Hale House Report described the loving environment, consistency and dedication which helps us to successfully meet the needs of children born addicted to drugs. However, every now and then, even our valiant efforts to "help children grow" cannot save them from the effects of narcotics, alcohol and AIDS.

This segment describes a battle lost, both for us and for a five-month-old infant named Danny.

Danny was born in June, 1988, to a substance-abusing woman in her thirties. Danny had four older siblings, all of whom were in foster care.

His mother sold "crack" and abused both crack and alcohol throughout her pregnancy with Danny. Because of her drug abuse, Danny was born four weeks prematurely and weighed only three pounds. Blood tests at birth revealed Danny's prenatal exposure to the purified form of cocaine (crack) and that both he and his mother had the AIDS virus.

Danny remained hospitalized until he was six pounds (August 1988), at which time he became a part of our Hale House family.

Danny's small, frail stature gave him the appearance of a newborn infant, even though he was already two months old. His facial features were similar to other children with fetal alcohol effects. The broad flat nose and very wide-set eyes were graphic reminders of his mother's use of alcohol during her pregnancy. Danny always seemed to have a very pained expression on his face.

He never smiled.

I don't mean as a young infant, I mean in his entire life. For the time that Danny lived at Hale House, he never smiled. His eating never improved. He continually threw up everything he ate. He functioned about as well as the average newborn. He cried incessantly. We massaged him, we exercised him, we cuddled him and we swaddled him. No matter what we did for Danny, nothing helped.

He continued to cry, maintained that pained expression on his face and sometimes stared into our eyes with such intensity that we wondered what secrets he knew about himself and about us as well.

Toward the end of October, Danny's health began to deteriorate. He ate less and less. His breathing was often labored, and he often wheezed during the night. He wasn't gaining weight. He was a frequent visitor to the emergency room at Harlem Hospital, arriving with symptoms as easy to treat as rashes and as hard to treat as his inability to gain weight.

By early November, Danny was admitted to Harlem Hospital because we knew there was nothing more we could do for him. The doctors tried everything. They gave him medication. They gave him a brain scan. They fed him intravenously. His mother spent time cuddling him in the hospital. But nothing helped.

Danny died on November 16, 1988, just two days after he turned five months old. He weighed six pounds when he died.

And he never smiled.

Why did we lose the battle with Danny? It wasn't AIDS. It was drugs. Had the drugs not destroyed his little body when he was in his mother's womb, he might have lived long enough to die from AIDS. But he never had the chance.

His brief, unhappy life reminds us here at Hale House that we must continue to fight the battle against drugs and drug addiction so that the Dannys of the world stand half a chance. Let us all be reminded that drugs, not just AIDS, kill.

And Danny never smiled.

# CHAPTER ELEVEN
## NED

If I had to pick a single story that best exemplifies the devastating influence of drug abuse on a young life, it has to be the story of Ned.

Ned came to us when he was four months old. His mother was an intravenous drug user and had recently become too ill to care for him. She had three other boys who her mother agreed to care for until she could take them back. However, the grandmother felt she simply could not manage an infant, too. Ned's father and mother were estranged at the time and though not a drug user himself, the father could not take Ned. So he came to Hale House.

We'd had him for seven months when he developed a bright rash on his back. It defied the usual remedies so we had further tests done to determine its cause.

I was sitting in my office looking over at City College. (The magnificence of its structure never fails to awe me—old Gothic lines, white brick accentuating the gray, steeples abound, truly a design of architectural significance.)

The phone rang. It was Ms. Edmond, the social worker.

"Dr. Hale, I've just received a call from the hospital. Ned has tested positive on the ELIZA screening test for the HIV-III/LAV antibody."

I couldn't speak.

"Dr. Hale, did you hear me?"

"Let me get back to you." I said, when her words registered, "What, what did you say? Ned? He's only eleven months old, he's just learning to walk."

"Yes, Ned is HIV positive," she replied.

I carefully placed the receiver down and looked again at City College, but this time my attention was on Ned.

That day was the seventh time Ms. Edmond had called to tell me:

"Dr. Hale, so-and-so has the antibody for the AIDS virus."

It was Friday, and just hours earlier Ned had left Hale House to spend the weekend with his father. Other than the persistent rash, Ned seemed well and healthy.

Before we could contact his father with the news, he called mid-day Saturday to inform us that Ned had been taken ill Friday night and had been admitted to the hospital with pneumonia. Mother Hale and I talked and recalled that besides his stubborn rash, he periodically "ran" fevers.

I guess we already knew the truth deep down, but didn't want to face it. We called the doctor and requested the AIDS antibody testing. After all, the baby had not had a cold, wasn't sneezing, nor had a runny nose. The diagnosis was suspect.

The following Thursday, Ned was released from the hospital and returned to Hale House. I decided to go to the residence, first to visit with Ned and then to discuss the situation with the staff.

When I entered the nursery, Ned greeted me, barely able to walk. He toddled over to me and raised his arms. I picked him up, kissed his cheek and gave him a squeeze.

My goodness! I thought, he is the cutest child. Large, almond-shaped black eyes, straight black hair, chubby cheeks just made for kisses, round button nose and a puckered mouth always ready for a smile or laughter. I was thinking, AIDS? He's just learning to walk.

"No, they're wrong," I said to myself.

When he began to wiggle to get down, I put him on the floor, where he stood momentarily to ensure his balance, then toddled off.

I asked his workers to meet with me. We talked about the situation; that is, AIDS and how it is spread. I told them that Ned needed another screening test, the Western Blot, for confirmation of the disease. Meanwhile, Ned should remain at Hale House.

To my surprise and pleasure the staff agreed!

Specific plans were made for his care. The nurses agreed to take a more active role in his daily activities, maintaining him in quasi-isolation, so that he would not contact diseases from the other children.

The plan worked for three months. The flu had hit Harlem hard that year and it found its way into Hale House. Ned got it and took a turn for the worse. His resistance too low to fight it off, we had to return Ned to the hospital into one of those rooms with the brightly colored cards tacked to the door that read: "CONTAMINATED."

It helped to a degree. He got over the flu but then he began to lose weight and had occasional seizures because the disease was affecting some part of his brain.

By that time, his mother had been officially diagnosed with AIDS and was dying in the same hospital. His grandmother and three brothers would have nothing to do with either his mother or Ned. His only visiting family member was his father, who came twice daily before and after work.

His other frequent visitor was my mother. Like the Good Shepherd of the Psalms, she'd leave "her flock" to see this one who was lost from her care and at the hospital. There were times we'd drop in to find his dad sitting beside him on the bed. Snuggled underneath his father's arm as his dad read him a story, Ned was like a sponge soaking up every bit of human contact he could touch...or should I say, that would touch him. Though failing rapidly, Ned lived for the visits from his father and Mother Hale.

Mother would always bring bright balloons and a small something to provide him some entertainment in his isolation. And she always brought plenty of hugs and kisses to help sustain his love-hungry spirit.

His mother died.

Drug abuse had claimed the first of not two, but three, lives. Enroute from work to visit Ned at the hospital, his father had entered a check cashing store to cash his paycheck. While inside, two gunmen entered to rob the store and randomly shot him and took his money. He died at the scene from a bullet wound to the head. Both gunmen were drug addicts, stealing to support their habit.

Mother had to break the news to the dying boy. When told of his father's death, the light in Ned's eyes that had resisted the ill winds of repeated infections, was extinguished by the tears he cried. He died within the week.

As I write this from my office, I gaze out once more at City College. Who knows, if Ned's life hadn't been touched by drug abuse, he might have been a student there pursuing a career as a researcher to find the cure for AIDS.

# NO ONE HEARD—NO ONE CARED

### By Gayle Tauger

*Bruised, O! little ones,*
*No one heard the anguished whimpers,*
*Yet the scars are ancient tattoos.*

*A smile will disfigure your battered face,*
*As your barren eyes seek final peace.*

*An innocent life mercifully seeking eternity,*
*Your presence a darkened void.*

*Little ones of fragile frame,*
*I kiss the softness of your soul,*
*I embrace the gentleness of your nature,*
*I hold your limp hand within my own.*

*Your memory, tho loving,*
*Still, a painful reminder that no one heard.*
*How shallow the screams become,*
*Merely utterances for survival.*

*Bruised, O! little ones,*
*You were here, your existence was.*
*Someone does care, you touched a heart.*
*Your life had meaning.*

*I sit here and mourn*
*For those of you who may still pass this way.*
*Perhaps, this time, someone will hear.*

# CHAPTER TWELVE
## LINDA

It was April 1985, and Mother Hale and I had been on the go for several months trying to raise public awareness and funding for Hale House.

That February during President Reagan's State of the Union Address, he recognized Mother and Hale House's first fifteen years of service. We went together to attend. It was amazing to realize that in those fifteen years we had cared for and saved the lives of more than 650 infants born addicted to heroin, methadone, cocaine and other drugs.

The national exposure had thrust us into the public's view and the recognition could not have been more timely. The presence of AIDS and crack/cocaine spreading through America's drug culture was creating a challenge we simply could not meet.

Hospitals were understaffed and lacked space (as they still do) for the escalating numbers of children born addicted to crack and/or HIV infected. Likewise, Hale House was too small and lacked both the manpower and medical facilities these children required.

Most people thought the crisis of caring for these children was approaching our nation's doorstep. But we knew firsthand that children had been crossing the threshold of our nation's door for years. Thousands were dying inside hospitals throughout the country.

Grateful that someone had drawn attention to what we were trying to do, it gave Mother Hale and me the opportunity to speak out on how serious the AIDS and drug epidemics already were. If we didn't wake up as a nation and address the devastating and deadly consequences of drug abuse, like "Proverbial Rome," we were destined to be destroyed from within.

Okay, off my soapbox and back to my story. Like I said, Mother and I had been traveling for months. Homebodies at heart, returning to Hale House was a welcomed hiatus for both of us. We missed our family of diapered darlings. Being back with them was a vacation to us.

I was driving home, still tired from the physical drag of jet lag. My mind wandered to the ongoing, often violent, battles between the pro-lifers and pro-choicers, the arguments against and for involuntary sterilization amid cries of genocide and protectionism.

I don't know the answers, nor do I want to enter into either controversy. But frequently, when I'm tired, the pain of the plight of the infants with whom I work becomes too much. As I often did, I began to think of Linda, our first baby diagnosed with AIDS.

There I was yesterday sitting beside the crib in the hospital looking at her. She'd gotten chubby, hands once so slim were now dimply, her cheeks fat. My, she had grown.

It had only been a year since Mother Hale and

I had been persuaded by Mrs. Helena Grey, Linda's mother, to care for her baby when it was born. Three months later, Mrs. Grey called and said she had given birth to a five-pound nine-ounce baby girl named Linda and that traces of cocaine had been found in the baby's urine. Therefore, the baby could not be released to her.

I asked our social worker to verify Mrs. Grey's statement with the hospital's Pediatrics Social Services and also to indicate that Hale House would care for Linda.

Mother and I knew Mrs. Grey well since we had cared for her other two boys, each of whom had become increasingly disturbed as they matured. They now attended special schools and lived with their maternal grandmother who was too old and too ill to care for them adequately. During her frequent illnesses, the boys were cared for by their two older brothers. These two oldest brothers had spent the majority of their lives in residential homes for disturbed children.

Appropriate arrangements were made, and after three months in the hospital, Linda was released to us. The prolonged hospitalization was necessary because her urine also revealed the presence of heroin, methadone and alcohol in addition to the cocaine. Furthermore, she was plagued with a continuous high fever.

Mother and I had been away during some of her developmental milestones. I was sorry I'd missed seeing her cut her two front teeth. It's such fun checking everyday to see if the teeth have finally come through. In my absence, she had begun to pull herself up while holding onto the crib.

It took two months after her arrival at Hale House for all the symptoms of drug withdrawal to disappear. Thin and sickly, mostly with colds and fevers, Linda had to be seen at the local clinic at least once a week.

She and Mother had a special relationship going that included various games. When Mother called her name, her eyes, so alert, would brighten and widen. I laughed and laughed at her reaction. It was always the same, no matter how many times they played it.

Aside from happy moments like those, she was very uncomfortable between cold sweats, fever, vomiting and crying for a bottle. If left in the crib, she rubbed her heels and elbows on the sheet until they were red. We took turns holding her most of the time, though Mother Hale seemed to get more of her than the rest of us. Feeding and holding her seemed somewhat of a comfort to Linda.

The one visible sign of a medical abnormality was an inexplicable extended stomach, similar to that of a severely malnourished child. It is referred to as "prune belly" and had only recently been determined as a birth defect peculiar to babies of mothers who used cocaine while pregnant.

Up until she was six months old, Linda's crib had been kept in Mother Hale's room. Then she was moved into the nursery when she had gained enough weight and her health had improved.

Her weight was slowly increasing, but her delightful behavior and disposition remained constant. She had won a place for herself in the hearts of all who knew her.

When she was seven months old, during one of several hospitalizations because of high fever, it was discovered that Linda was unable to eliminate sufficient amounts of bodily waste, causing her continual discomfort and bloatedness. The condition was corrected, and her protruding stomach disappeared.

However, a month later, during another hospital stay, our social worker was told that Linda's blood revealed the AIDS antibodies, indicating that she had been exposed to the AIDS virus. Linda was to be our first AIDS baby.

As loved as she was among the staff, the fear of AIDS overrode that love initially. They did not want her to return to Hale House. They saw it as too great a risk to the other children as well as fear of contracting AIDS themselves. Mother and I were dismayed by their unmovable stance.

I offered arguments. I pleaded. I tried to make them feel guilty, but they were adamant. Finally, I asked if Linda was different now than she had been during the five months she had lived at Hale House.

"We know," was the response.

"But," I insisted, "you kissed her, hugged her, changed her Pampers, bathed her, loved her. . . she's no different now.''

''No, she isn't different. We are, because now we know,'' was the reply.

I prevailed.

Linda did return to Hale House and was placed in an isolated room. One child-care worker virtually moved into Hale House and took care of her for the following two weeks. No one else went near her. Then, another high fever, another hospitalization. But this time everyone was prepared. We knew the problem. Those not afraid looked in on Linda and acknowledged her as still the adorable little girl she was.

People's reaction to Linda because of her diagnosis was understandable in light of being misinformed or ignorant of the nature of AIDS. But, in another way, it was inexcusable when you stop and think, ''How must that child feel to suddenly go from being lovable and huggable to 'you are untouchable?''' It broke Mother's and my heart. And from Linda's experience we were determined to somehow help infant victims of AIDS.

Linda was kept in isolation at the hospital right up to her first birthday. Between our duties at Hale House, Mother and I took turns visiting her as often as we could. Just the three of us celebrated her birthday. I remember how thrilled she was to have us arrive together. To have more than one person to play with at the same time was a birthday present in itself. Linda was beside herself.

Mother and I came with red balloons, her

favorite color. We'd picked up some cupcakes from a bakery and little ice cream cups from the hospital snack shop. But the best thing of all was the stuffed white bear Mother had picked out. Not only was it the softest and most cuddly one we could find, but when you pressed its tummy it would record what you said and then play it back to you.

Mother and I recorded our voices on it for her and showed her how to press its tummy. She didn't have the strength to push hard enough so we kept doing it for her. She was captivated by it.

We must have sung "Happy Birthday" a dozen times for the bear to play it back. It was finally time to go. As we left, she waved goodbye while hugging tightly to her talking bear.

Standing by the door, I contemplated the innocence of babies and wondered if Linda would ever know that a world existed beyond her hospital room. A world with laughing children, teasing adolescents and caring adults. I wondered if Linda would ever see a playground, experience a swing, a see-saw, climb a Jungle Jim or attend a school.

As we walked down the corridor to the elevator, I noticed there were more doors with orange-red cards on which were written the word "CONTAMINATED." A nurse with a mask, head covering, gown and rubber gloves was removing a red plastic refuse bag marked "CONTAMINATED" from one of the rooms.

There were eight infant AIDS victims on the ward at that time. Each baby was alone in a room, the youngest only three months old. The majority of them were totally abandoned by their mothers and now considered wards of the state.

So much confusion, so much fear. And here these little ones, so innocent, so vulnerable, depending on us, the adults, to protect them, and we are powerless. I wanted to cry. But I was too overwhelmed—by drugs—by AIDS—by feeling powerless.

But then I thought of what Mother Hale had taught me was the "secret ingredient" to turning a bitter situation into a sweeter one: love. It was really all Mother and I had in the beginning to offer that first baby in 1969. And it was what we'd been giving the over 800 babies since. Yes, it had worked wonders in the past. It wouldn't fail us now.

"Love really is a force all its own," I thought to myself. Tender love has the ability to soothe a feverish baby going through withdrawal, while fierce love can stand up and fight for the rights of a baby with AIDS to be treated with dignity and compassion.

"Yes, love in action is stronger than all the forces of fear, hate, ignorance and apathy," my inner voice shouted.

Right then and there I purposed that just as Hale House had always opened its doors to children born addicted to drugs, we would also open our arms to innocent babies born with AIDS. Love would find a way.

I submitted a proposal to the child welfare department for permission and assistance to open a home for young children with AIDS. After waiting a reasonable amount of time, we called and called, confident only some minor delay was holding up their approval.

Our proposal was the only one of its kind and the only one submitted to the New York City Child Welfare Administration. We were a natural pick to work with these special children because of our success with those born addicted to drugs and those with AIDS. Though not all children exposed to drugs in the womb have AIDS, it's very likely that children born with AIDS have also been exposed to drugs. It was a terrible blow when we were informed eight months later that funding had been granted to another agency. Their proposal was so similar to ours that we were suspect!

It's been three years since that night I drove home pondering Linda's little life. We had no idea that she would live to reach a second birthday, much less a third. But she has.

Unfortunately, the time bomb called AIDS ticking inside her little body was not her most deadly problem.

Her father was.

We had known since the day we took Linda home from the hospital that even though her mother was a junkie, her father was really "bad news."

Helena never talked a lot about "her old man," but when she did, a cold fear would grip her face. She warned us every time she contacted us to never, ever let her father take her from Hale House.

We heard her words of warning, but when the father started legal steps to gain custody of Linda, there was nothing we could do. He and his new lady friend had showed up at Hale House a few times for a visit all dressed up to the nines and smelling of too much cologne.

We tolerated the visits, and hoped that would be the end of it. Then one Monday morning before we'd even fed the children their breakfast, they showed up with all the right paperwork to take Linda "home."

With a very heavy heart, we handed our poor sick darling over to them.

Less than 3 months later the child was found drowned in the couple's bathtub. Tests showed she had bruises over most of her frail body and even her spleen was damaged.

Whatever happened to Helena? The last we heard, she had called this terrible man and asked permission to attend her own daughter's funeral.

He said "no."

# WHAT BIRDS
# AND CHILDREN KNOW

"I need wide spaces in my heart,
Where faith and I can go apart,
and grow serene.
Life gets so choked by busy living,
Kindness so lost in fussy giving,
That love slips by unseen.

I want to make a quiet place,
Where those I love can see God's face,

Can stretch their hearts across the earth,
Can understand what Spring is worth:

Can count the stars;
Watch violets grow,
And learn what birds and children know."

From: The Scottish Recorder 1930

# CHAPTER THIRTEEN
## MY DREAM

The preceding poem, "What Birds and Children Know" describes a special dream I've carried in my heart for years. It's a special dream because it is for special children. Children who themselves haven't very long to dream.

In the past twenty-two years of working with children born to drug abusing mothers, I've seen a lot of suffering on the part of those children. But following withdrawal, most of the physical suffering ends and with speech or physical therapy many of them can go on to live productive lives.

But since the advent of AIDS, things have changed drastically for the worse. Suffering for these children begins at birth and ends only with death. What time there is in between is so brief, it simply shouldn't be wasted.

Yet, because many of these children are abandoned either before or because they are diagnosed with AIDS, they are left in hospitals to live out their days in isolation and loneliness.

Thousands of other children are terminally ill with cancer or leukemia or suffering with life-threatening conditions such as a diseased heart or liver. They, too, are confined to the stark and impersonal environment of a hospital for weeks, months and sometimes years.

Often, the only companionship they have is a

television set or a few toys to play with. They see the doctors and nurses and maybe — maybe an occasional visitor or volunteer, brave or caring enough to give them a hug or kiss.

All children deserve so much more. They deserve the right to be children, discovering and exploring life. And they deserve to die with dignity and surrounded with people who know them and love them, instead of just strangers taking care of them until they die.

I dream of these children having a place especially for them. A place where they can be in touch with the world as God made it before high-rises and subways.

A place where terminally ill children can live what time they have left on this earth. . .close to the earth, beholding the wonder and beauty and glory of nature.

Most specifically, I want this place to be for children born in metropolitan cities. Children who otherwise will never know a robin or a blue jay or know the feel of grass beneath their feet instead of concrete and pavement.

Children who, otherwise, will never inhale the fragrance of honeysuckle or freshly cut grass or hear the song of a sparrow or chirp of a cricket. Because they are destined to only know the antiseptic smell of a hospital or, if allowed outside, air choked with pollution. Familiar sounds to them will only be voices of strangers over a hospital intercom or sirens and car horns blaring outside.

My dream includes wide-open spaces to play, gardens to learn to grow things, a pond to skip rocks across and go fishing in. There would be paths to take walks along and perhaps even a small barn where children can be taught to care for animals.

It will be a facility capable of handling the children's medical needs yet also offer more of a "home" type atmosphere than a hospital. The staff will include doctors, nurses, childcare workers, teachers and volunteers who love children and are dedicated to helping and challenging them to discover their world before they leave it.

It will not be a place to sit, stare, and die, but a place to touch, feel, see, hear, smell and experience life as long as life is theirs to live.

My dream includes a round building with a garden in the center. Every child's room will look out towards the garden area so they can always see trees and birds and watch the seasons change.

I've seen too many children in recent years who have no will to live because they had no reason to live, no place to go, nobody to live for. Their existence is as sterile as the walls of a hospital. Many of them die desperately lonely, emotionally starved for someone to touch them, read to them, teach them all the things a child needs to learn. These precious innocent children are dying daily never knowing somebody loved them.

I share my dream with you in hopes you will dream it, too, and help me make it come true.

My heart's desire has been, and always will be,

to see the work of Hale House continue. Hale House must continue. . .until pregnant women stop taking drugs. . .until venereal diseases are eradicated. . .and until a cure is found for AIDS.

Yes, yes, yes! Hale House must continue to help the innocent victims of these life-threatening forces. As long as there are babies in need of love and care, Hale House must be here to meet their needs.

And when it is certain that a child is going to die, we want to have a place for them where dying isn't lonely or sad, but just part of living, just part of growing old—even if old is only the age of three. Unlike Don Quixote's impossible dream, I believe my dream is possible. It isn't a dream of reaching the "unreachable star" he speaks of. It is simply a dream that, if accomplished, will help fulfill the final days of dying children. The dream of providing a place where little ones. . .

"Can count the stars;
Watch violets grow,
And learn what birds and children know."

# CHAPTER FOURTEEN

## "SEE ME"

In 1990, in the United States, over 375,000 children were born addicted to drugs. Hundreds of thousands of these were also infected in the womb with venereal diseases or AIDS.

Crack/cocaine is one of the most popular illegal drugs among Americans. Second only to the legal drug, alcohol, it can be devastating to in-utero development. While causing some severe physical problems, the greater damage is initially invisible. As these crack/cocaine-exposed babies mature, researchers and doctors are discovering some neurological impairment in their mental and emotional development. More and more babies are being abandoned by women who enter the hospital to give birth and walk out hours later, leaving their newborn with an adult-size drug addiction. One that will take it weeks or months to withdraw from.

Many of these babies are also destined to die from AIDS. And the numbers are in epidemic proportion to the number of facilities and personnel trained to deal with this "plague of the '90s." A plague that is creating a generation of "invisible" and "untouchable" children.

By the very fact that you are reading this book, you must believe, as we do so deeply, that these children do not deserve to suffer. That the injustice of drug abuse in the womb, and the hideous disease of AIDS that courses through their blood, is unfair.

You must believe, along with us, that any effort to ease their pain is noble. . .and worth supporting.

However you feel about AIDS, please understand that this is not a moral issue. The issue we must address is how to ease the suffering of children and help them to live out their painfully short lives in peace.

They deserve that from us. . .all of us. These infants have so little time to stay on this earth. Help us to make it a time of love, comfort, and joy.

These children are victims. Totally and utterly helpless victims of their mothers' actions. And though addicted or infected, they are children. Children who "but for the grace of. . ." could be you or me.

We all know how children will say, "Watch me! Watch me!" or "Did you see me?" They thrive on being noticed and affirmed.

Yet, there are thousands of children crying the same words. . ."See me!" Crying from behind the bars of an institutional crib. . ."See me!" Crying from tender hearts. . ."See me, see me!"

Children, like all children that yearn to be touched, yearn to be held and told, "Yes, I see you! Yes, you're wonderful. Yes, I love you and I'm glad you're here."

At Hale House we are listening to their cries. For that matter, we were very likely the only ones listening back in the late '60s when we took in our first drug-exposed baby. All these years we've been charting the course of childcare for these special children and discovering their unique needs. Our foundational knowledge is firm and vast, thanks to experience we've gained in caring for hundreds of children over the past two decades.

But to continue our work at Hale House, we need friends and funding to keep the doors opened. We firmly feel and believe that to fully implement our knowledge of how to care for the whole child, we must be an agency that is self-governed. At Hale House, we aren't out to become the "biggest," but we do want to be "our best" for the children.

We do not want to sacrifice our successful strategies learned over the years and high standards of childcare that have made such an impact on the lives of those we care for and who work at Hale House. It's no secret that bureaucratic policy tied to government funding tends to encumber and erode effectiveness and performance. We don't want that to happen at Hale House. The children we help are too deserving, too needy, too precious, to receive anything less than the best we can give them as a care agency.

I ask you now to recall the various stories you've just read and consider the questions, "What if you had been born Thomas. . .or Delcia. . .or any one of these children you've read about? What if your life had begun the way theirs did? Would you want Hale House to be there for you?"

If your answer is yes, I ask you to put your affirmation into action by sending as generous a gift as possible. And do it today, before you have a chance to forget any of the true stories I've shared with you. And also, decide to commit yourself to send regular monthly support to help us take the giant and necessary step towards self-sufficiency.

If this book accomplishes anything, I pray it opens the eyes and ears and hearts of caring people like you, who will see these children, hear their cries, and help us tell them and show them they are "seen," that they are loved, and that we are here for them.

Help us love them while we can. Help us not let a single child die without him or her knowing we were glad they lived.

Please, don't forget these children.

Send your most generous gift today!

From all of us at Hale House, thank you for reading this little book. Thank you for giving. And, God bless you.

# EPILOGUE

It's been over two decades and close to a thousand children since that first baby kept Mother Hale and I up all night...night after night...for five weeks.

Pioneering the care of babies born to drug-addicted mothers has been challenging, frustrating, exhausting and above all, rewarding. Oh, yes, it's been a lot of things, but never boring.

We've had to work hard to hold a steady course in unchartered waters. Our only compass in the beginning was the one in our hearts. It pointed straight to God's word in Psalms 82:3-4 which says, "Defend the cause of the weak and fatherless; maintain the rights of the poor and oppressed. Rescue the weak and needy."

To do that, it costs something—your time, your energy, your money, your love.

It's those things that have made Hale House, "The House That Love Built" a reality. It was established and has been maintained by people willing to live the conviction that every child deserves the love and dignity he or she is inherently due as a human being.

Modifying the company slogan, "Babies are our business," I submit to you that the children of our nation, regardless of color, physical or mental attributes, parentage, or where they live, are our business.

At Hale House, we're committed to care for and love all God's children. We believe that those children with drugs coursing through their newborn bodies especially need our love, along with children diagnosed with AIDS, whether simply carrying the HIV virus or sick and dying with AIDS.

Babies don't give themselves drugs, or syphilis, or AIDS. And they are no less worthy of being loved and cared for than a healthy child. If anything, they need to be affirmed of their worth in a greater way because of their afflictions.

Help us show them they are precious. Help us show them they are valuable and their lives matter. Help us love them whether their lives are brief or last a full lifetime.

Help us. . .help us love them.

Send your best gift to:
   Hale House
   68 Edgecombe Avenue
   New York, NY 10030

*Hale House: The House That Love Built* is a moving account of the remarkable history of this home for drug-addicted babies.

Hale House is a non-profit organization that depends on the free will gifts of support from its friends.

Please help if you can.

---

☐ Yes! I want to help the babies at Hale House. Here is my gift of:

☐ $10 _____    ☐ $25 _____    $ 100 _____    Other _____

Name _____

Address _____

City _____ State _____ Zip _____

BK91

Share the story of Hale House with a friend.

We believe that the more people are aware of the problems in society that are causing so many children to be born addicted to drugs, the sooner we can begin to solve the problem.

After you read this book, please pass it along to a friend. If you would like more copies, just fill out this coupon and return it to us. And know that because you took the time to care, a precious child has a loving home.

Please send me _____ copies of *Hale House: The House That Love Built.* To help defray the cost of sending you these books, we request a minimum donation of $3 per book. Please allow 6-8 weeks for delivery.

Name _____

Address _____

City _____ State _____ Zip _____

BK91

Please send your tax-deductible gift to:
  Hale House
  68 Edgecombe Avenue
  New York, NY 10030